MARRIAGE ISN'T FOR YOU

It's for the One You Love

For Kim:
Marriage still isn't for me.
I'm yours.

All photographs and illustrations throughout the book are used by permission. Page vi-vii © Rock and Wasp/ Shutterstock.com; page viii © Michael Jung/Shutterstock.com; page 3 © Matthew Nigel/Shutterstock.com; page 4 © Rido/Shutterstock.com; page 7 © Pavel Vakhrushev/Shutterstock.com; page 8 © Nicolesa/Shutterstock.com; page 11 © Umkehrer/Shutterstock.com; page 12 © dotshock/Shutterstock.com; page 17 © VannPhotography/Shutterstock .com; page 18 © Kate Benson Photography; page 20-21 © Peter Bernik/Shutterstock.com; page 23 © Andrey Arkusha/Shutterstock.com; page 24 © Kichigin/Shutterstock.com; page 27 © Eugene Sergeev/Shutterstock .com; page 28 © takayuki/Shutterstock.com; page 31 © gpointstudio/Shutterstock.com; page 32 © Ruth Black/ Shutterstock.com; page 35 © wavebreakmedia/Shutterstock.com; page 36 © nenetus/Shutterstock.com; page 39 © Phaendin/Shutterstock.com.

Visit us at ShadowMountain.com

Library of Congress Cataloging-in-Publication Data

Smith, Seth Adam, author.
  Marriage isn't for you / Seth Adam Smith.
    pages cm
  ISBN 978-1-60907-902-4 (hardbound : alk. paper) 1. Marriage. I. Title.
  HQ734.S745 2014
  306.81—dc23   2014005265

Printed in Canada
Friesens, Manitoba, Canada

10 9 8 7 6 5 4 3 2 1

MARRIAGE

isn't

FOR YOU

It's for the One You Love

SETH ADAM SMITH

SHADOW
MOUNTAIN

· Thinking of You ·

*I met my wife in high school, when
we were both fifteen years old.
We were friends for ten years, until . . .
until we decided we no longer
wanted to be just friends. :)*

I STRONGLY RECOMMEND THAT BEST FRIENDS FALL IN LOVE.

fear

*Nevertheless, falling
in love with my best friend
did not prevent me from
having certain*

FEARS AND ANXIETIES

about getting married.

*The nearer Kim and I
approached the decision to
marry, the more I was filled
with a paralyzing fear.*

WAS I READY?

WAS I MAKING THE
RIGHT CHOICE?

WAS KIM THE RIGHT
PERSON TO MARRY?

WOULD SHE MAKE
ME HAPPY?

Then, one fateful night,
I shared these thoughts and
concerns with my dad.

Perhaps all of us have moments
in our lives when it feels like
time slows down or the air becomes
still and everything around us seems
to draw in, marking that moment
as one we will never forget.

My dad's response
to my concerns created such
a moment for me.

With a knowing smile, he said,

"SETH, YOU'RE BEING TOTALLY SELFISH.

SO I'M GOING TO MAKE THIS REALLY SIMPLE:

MARRIAGE ISN'T FOR YOU.

"You don't marry to make yourself happy, you marry to make someone else happy.

More than that, your marriage isn't for yourself— you're marrying for a family.

Not just for the in-laws and all of that nonsense, but for your
FUTURE CHILDREN.

?

"WHO DO YOU WANT TO HELP YOU RAISE THEM?

WHO DO YOU WANT TO INFLUENCE THEM?

Marriage isn't for you.
It's not about you. Marriage is
about the person you marry."

IN THAT MOMENT,

I KNEW
THAT SHE
WAS THE
"RIGHT"
PERSON
TO MARRY.

I realized that I wanted to make
her happy, to see her smile every day,
to make her laugh every day.

I wanted to be a part
of her family, and my family
wanted her to be a part of ours.

And thinking back on all the
times I had seen her play with
my nieces, I knew that
SHE WAS THE ONE
with whom I wanted
to build our own family.

MY FATHER'S ADVICE WAS BOTH SHOCKING AND REVELATORY.

It went against the grain of a world that demands self-fulfillment over self-sacrifice; a world that says you can "have it all" but scoffs at the idea of marriage and family

BEING IT ALL;

a world that subscribes to the idea that relationships are as temporal as a purchase at the supermarket— if it doesn't make you happy, you can take it back and get a new one.

marriage

NO, A TRUE MARRIAGE
(WITH TRUE LOVE)
IS NEVER ABOUT YOU.

IT'S ABOUT THE
PERSON YOU LOVE—
THAT PERSON'S

*WANTS, NEEDS,
HOPES,
AND DREAMS.*

SELFISHNESS DEMANDS,
"What's in it for me?"

♥

LOVE ASKS,
"What can I give?"

Some time ago,

MY WIFE SHOWED ME WHAT IT MEANS TO LOVE SELFLESSLY.

· ·

FOR MANY MONTHS, MY HEART HAD BEEN HARDENING WITH A MIXTURE OF FEAR AND RESENTMENT.

Then, after the pressure
had built up to where
neither of us could stand
it, emotions erupted.

I WAS
CALLOUS.

I WAS
SELFISH.

But instead of matching my selfishness, Kim did something beyond wonderful—she showed an outpouring of love.

Laying aside all of the pain and anguish that I had caused her, she lovingly took me in her arms and soothed my soul.

I REALIZED THAT I HAD FORGOTTEN MY DAD'S ADVICE.

While Kim's side of the marriage had been to love me, my side of the marriage had become all about me.

This awful realization brought me to tears. I got on my knees and promised my wonderful wife that I would try to be better.

To all who read this book—

MARRIED,

ALMOST MARRIED,

SINGLE,

OR EVEN THE
SWORN BACHELOR

OR BACHELORETTE—

*I want you to know that
marriage isn't for you.
No true relationship of love
is for you. Love is about
the person you love.*

PARADOXICALLY,

the more you truly love that person, the more love you receive. And not just from your significant other, but from his or her friends and family and thousands of others you never would have met had your love remained self-centered.

TRULY, MARRIAGE ISN'T FOR YOU.

Love isn't for you.

LOVE IS FOR THE ONE YOU LOVE.

YOU ARE PART
OF MY EXISTENCE,
PART OF MYSELF.

—CHARLES DICKENS

Great Expectations

Coming in September 2014 from Seth Adam Smith

YOUR LIFE ISN'T FOR YOU

A SELFISH PERSON'S GUIDE TO BEING SELFLESS

Now that you know marriage "isn't for you," Seth Adam Smith has some news: nothing in your life is. In this inspiring, funny, and moving book, Seth shows how a philosophy of living for others can enrich every aspect of your life, just as it has his.

Seth reveals how, years before his marriage, his selfishness led to a downward spiral of addiction and depression, culminating in a suicide attempt at the age of 20. It was the love and support he experienced in the aftermath, which Seth so poignantly depicts here, that opened his eyes to this new outlook.

As he reflects on his life—a difficult year in Russia, his time as a youth leader in the Arizona desert, his marriage, even a story his father read to him when he was a child—he shares his conviction, born of these experiences, that the only way to live your life is to give it to others.

Berrett–Koehler Publishers, Inc.
www.bkconnection.com
800.929.2929

$12.95, paperback
ISBN 978-1-62656-095-6